Several True (I Think) Stories:

Can Truth Be Stranger Than Fiction?

Second Edition

Published by James E. Gibson, Freelance Writer
Lexington, KY

James E. Gibson

Second Edition published April 23, 2017, with a few minor changes made later in April 2017, and additional changes in September 2019.

Second Edition ISBN: 978-0-9988774-0-2

Second Edition LCCN: 2017905176

First Edition published June 10, 2016, with numerous small changes/corrections made on June 29, 2016.

Published by James E. Gibson, Freelance Writer

P.O. Box 54868, Lexington, KY 40555-4868

United States of America

E-mail: jamesegibson@gmail.com

You may contact the author at the address above. He appreciates all comments, questions, suggestions, etc., but cannot promise to provide everyone a personal reply.

About 35-40% of the stories included in this book are reprinted or adapted from stories printed in the author's first book, *True Christianity: It May Not Be What You Think* (2014, second edition 2015, third edition 2017). It is still available. Some of the stories have been published elsewhere, too.

Table of Contents

Acknowledgments

The highest righteous power, which I call God, deserves credit and glory for any good from this book. Without God I could do nothing, wouldn't even exist.

Thanks also to all my relatives, friends, neighbors, coworkers, and everyone else that I've encountered in my life for their help. They have helped me immensely in various ways over the years of my life thus far.

These individuals are too numerous to mention specifically by name. In fact, to help prevent persons from getting undesired publicity, I seldom mention names and specific personal information in the book. However, I love everyone and appreciate the positive roles everyone has played in my life.

Thank you all very much!

About the Front Cover

White symbolizes purity and unity. The colored horizontal lines represent diversity and add color to the cover. The blue book title symbolizes the heavens, sky, and God. The green subtitle and author name symbolize human greenness, limited knowledge. The purple edition number symbolizes the ministry of serving others, the ongoing progress to produce a better book. The simple cover I created (under God's leadership I hope) saved me the expense of hiring a professional cover designer—and enabled me to create the cover my (God's?) way.

Disclaimer

I believe all the stories in this book are true. Furthermore, I tried to present them without hyperbole, since I consider hyperbole a fancy word for lying.

Most of the events described in the book are based on my personal memories. I sought to be accurate and to express my opinions honestly in a relatively positive way. God deserves the credit to the extent that I succeeded. However, errors could occur due to my misunderstanding events originally when they happened, faulty personal memory, or errors in my writing.

In cases where the events described in the book are not personal experiences, but are events described to me by someone else or that I learned about through research of some type, errors could also occur due to incorrect information from my source(s) for whatever reason(s).

All the opinions expressed in this book are those of the author (me, James E. Gibson). They do not reflect the views of any other person or organization.

I love everyone and hope nothing I've written offends anyone.

During my life, I have experienced (and witnessed) a large number of very unusual things. If I hadn't personally experienced or witnessed them, I likely would not have believed many of them. Therefore, I certainly understand if readers don't believe some of the stories contained in this book.

Often true stories are so extraordinary that those who didn't experience or observe them firsthand find them unbelievable. Perhaps God endows us with enormous powers of hearing, seeing, thinking, etc., that we seldom develop or use as God desires.

A few stories in this book seem almost as miraculous as some of the miracles described in the Bible—and not always in a positive way. I decided not to include a few perhaps even more unbelievable incidents due to inability to sufficiently make the identities of others involved anonymous while detailing the stories.

I realize many readers will find even the incidents I included unbelievable. Still, I feel it is important to include them.

I've lived my entire life in Kentucky, and most of these incidents occurred in Kentucky. But, I think they could have happened elsewhere, too.

The chapters are numbered, but you may skip around and read the stories in any particular order.

I hope readers enjoy reading about these very unusual events—real events if my memory is correct.

To the best of my memory, they are all true stories, and I tried to describe them accurately, avoiding the use of hyperbole (exaggeration), which I consider a fancy word for lying when writing nonfiction, as I stated in the disclaimer that precedes this introduction.

Numerous unusual events occur daily. Some likely go unnoticed. It seems that I have been blessed by God to experience or witness an especially large number of unusual events and coincidences.

At least once I heard an inaudible voice stating that I was the best Jew baby in 2,000 years. I don't know exactly what a Jew baby is, and I didn't find it defined in the dictionary or adequately defined online either. And I have no idea if it is possible that I am a Jew baby or the best one in 2,000 years. That somehow makes me think the voice was seeking to compare me to Jesus. Who knows? At any rate, it was only an inaudible voice that I heard inside. I certainly don't claim to be the resurrected Jesus.

However, I firmly believe that all things occur for a reason. And, as we learn from our experiences and the experiences of others, we can make ourselves and our world better through the grace and guidance of God.

We are all blessed in various ways during our lifetimes. Each individual is given certain unique strengths that can enable him (or her) to cope effectively with the challenges he (or she) faces and to succeed under the guidance of what I call God, the highest righteous power.

Personally, I feel that God (as well as genetics, environment, education, etc.) gifts each of us in ways that no other individual is gifted. I seem to have some gifts I don't see in others. And I am confident that each person I have met has certain gifts that I lack. Chapter 38 titled "Disabilities and Abilities" discusses this a bit more.

I hope and pray that reading about the events described in this book helps each reader to act and react more constructively in the present and future than he or she has in the past. And I hope that I have learned things from the events I have experienced and witnessed that have made me a better person.

Focusing on positive thoughts, using positive words, and engaging in positive actions can be a constructive influence on our lives as well as the lives of those around us. Why do people go to war, lie, steal, etc.? What does it take to communicate the right thing to do to one another and to convince persons to do it? Maybe unusual events are a way God uses (or allows others to use) to guide us into doing the right things.

Please try to read about the incidents described in this book with an open mind. And I encourage you to e-mail me at jamesegibson@gmail.com with your comments, questions, and/or constructive criticism. I appreciate all comments, questions, and constructive criticism, but I can't promise to provide everyone a personal reply. Thanks.

I hope you find the book entertaining, informative, and inspiring. If so, God deserves the credit, not me.

Chapter 1: Witch's Fire?

Several years ago, on an occasion when I did volunteer work helping another person at a location in Kentucky I won't disclose, the other individual became frustrated and upset about something. Perhaps he felt that I wasn't helping enough. And I wasn't doing much; I lacked experience at the particular task and was unsure what to do.

Suddenly I saw what looked like a stream of fire in front of me. It looked like images I've seen on fictional television shows of fire coming from the mouths of fire-breathing dragons. Another person who was there said that the other person had made "witch's fire" come from my eyes.

I used the Google search engine to seek more information about "witch's fire," but was unsuccessful in finding a definition that seemed to fit. Maybe someday I'll do a more detailed search, God willing.

I don't know where the "fire" in this incident came from, but it did seem to be directly in front of me. It disappeared very quickly, perhaps as quickly as it appeared, and it apparently caused no damage. At least two of us saw it—or saw something. What was it? Could it have been an optical illusion?

I have read supposedly true stories about persons starting fires. If I ever start a fire with my eyes, I hope it is for a good purpose. And I don't feel that was a good purpose that day when I was doing volunteer work, and someone apparently accidentally caused "witch's fire" to come from my eyes, whatever "witch's fire" is.

Chapter 2: Eyes Heating a Wedding Ring to Burn a Finger?

At a time I won't disclose at a location in Kentucky I won't disclose (to help keep the person anonymous), I was working with a particular person. On one occasion, our hands accidentally touched as we worked, and I tried focusing my eyes on her wedding ring to reduce the attraction I felt toward her. However, my vision seemed a bit blurred for a brief period, so I couldn't. Then suddenly my eyes focused directly on her ring instantly, like they had been directed there by an outside power. I got the impression that she used some spiritual power to somehow help my eyes focus. But I don't know.

At any rate, I saw a flash of light and her wedding ring glowed like bright sunlight was reflecting off it. I blinked, then looked again to verify that it wasn't an illusion. The wedding ring still glowed. I was going to draw her attention to the unusual appearance of her ring. Before I could, she ran off to rinse her finger and told someone that her finger was burned, and James's eyes burned it.

Apparently somehow my eyes had focused on her ring in a way that caused the ring to get hot enough to burn her finger. I felt terrible about it. What caused that? Did she feel my attraction for her and/or feel attracted toward me and focus my eyes upon her ring to reduce the attraction? Who knows?

Although I personally have experienced many things that I consider answers to prayer, it is not easy to convince others that such things were answers to prayer. Even if I provided a huge list, you might attribute the answers to something other than prayer—or accuse me of lying. However, in some other chapters you will find a few examples of what I consider answers to prayers. And, in this chapter I provide two examples of what I considered answered prayers.

The first example comes from my college years. When I was in college at the University of Kentucky, a roommate often showered and blow dried his hair early in the morning, waking me up. I usually tolerated it good naturedly, since I typically went right back to sleep soon afterward and slept until either I awakened more normally or my alarm clock went off, and he was a fabulous roommate. One morning, however, I prayed something like, "God, if it be your will, please shut off that blow dryer." Very soon afterward, the blow dryer stopped operating. A few minutes later my roommate came in, shook me softly, and apologized for getting me up, but said his blow dryer had quit working and asked to borrow mine. God (or some unidentified force) certainly stopped that blow dryer.

My roommate coming in to disturb me a few minutes after the blow dryer quit (asking to borrow mine) may have been justice served to me for a somewhat selfish prayer. But if I remember correctly, on that day I didn't even own a blow dryer yet, since at that time I let my hair dry naturally after washing it, so his hair remained wet a while longer that day.

A second example of answered prayer occurred one day several years ago when I was shopping in a supermarket. I saw a baby left alone in a shopping cart by a lady who was probably the child's mother, while the woman went to get some item(s) in a nearby aisle of the store. The baby began moving around in the shopping cart's child seat, then suddenly climbed up and fell out, while the woman was several feet away and didn't see. I was too far away to run and catch the baby. I prayed. I prayed hard. The baby seemed to perform a triple somersault in the air before landing uninjured on its feet, even though it appeared too young to even walk. The startled woman returned to the cart unsure how the baby fell or landed uninjured. I considered it a "miracle" in answer to prayer.

In addition to the above two stories, there are numerous other apparent answers to prayer I have experienced. And as I stated earlier, some other chapters in the book discuss some of these cases.

One day when I was at work at a particular job, at a location in Kentucky that I won't disclose, a worker who normally dressed nicely in business apparel was wearing very short pants. I looked at her with disapproval of her apparel and probably a bit of lust.

She looked back at me from where she was standing, perhaps 15 or 20 feet away, and said something like, "I don't like the way James is looking at me. That's not like him. If he does it again, I'm going to hit him." I did it again, and then I felt a terrible eye pain, perhaps the worst I'd ever felt in my life. I prayed for relief if it was God's will. I prayed hard.

As I continued praying, a coworker ran up in front of me; she was a Pentecostal Christian. The pain instantly ended. She said something like, "There, is that better?" I said something like "yes, thank you, God." I am confident that God somehow relayed my silent prayers to that Pentecostal coworker who served as God's instrument to heal me.

Later, the person who said "I'm going to hit him" told someone else that she was glad that coworker helped me, that she would have removed that "curse" from me herself if she knew how since I appeared to be in such pain, but she didn't know how to do so. Apparently, one coworker put a "curse" on me, and another "healed" me. I considered it a "miraculous" healing.

In this chapter I discuss two personal experiences of "speaking in tongues." Neither of them occurred in a church.

One of the two times I "spoke in tongues" occurred when I was a patient in a psychiatric hospital in Kentucky. (I discuss my period of mental illness briefly in Chapter 34.) This incident of "speaking in tongues" occurred when one of the staff members in the hospital was questioning someone who replied to her question with a lie, and I interrupted the person who was lying to correct them.

The staff member looked at me and somehow did something that turned my words into gibberish. It was like she had figuratively twisted my tongue so that it wasn't moving the way I intended. The staff person then told me something like, "Now, be quiet, I'm talking to them right now." I don't know what the staff person did or how she did it, but somehow she altered my voice without touching me.

The other incident when I "spoke in tongues" occurred when I was in the yard of my dad and mom's house in Jenkins, Kentucky. I was speaking to my dad and another person. My thoughts were coming to me very quickly, and I was afraid I would forget my insights before I could express them, so I tried speaking faster and faster so I could convey them before I forgot them. Then somehow some "superhuman" power (God?) enabled me to speak very fast, so fast that my words sounded like gibberish, even though they were in English. I don't know how I managed to speak so fast that time. I was speaking with such speed that the other two people could not understand what I was saying.

I think these are the only two times that I ever spoke in tongues. I have visited some church services where others appeared to speak in tongues. But I don't know if they were speaking in unknown tongues, speaking English fast, speaking a foreign language, or faking it.

At any rate, the two incidents I described from my personal experience proved to me that "speaking in tongues" can occur. And I am confident there are cases where others have "spoken in tongues," maybe cases where the "speaking in tongues" has been very beneficial.

However, I felt that in both my personal experiences, the "speaking in tongues" was unnecessary. Had I not interrupted, the staff person would not have turned my words into gibberish in the first example. And if I had spoken slowly enough that my words could be understood, the second case would not have occurred.

Some claim that sexual orientation reversal is impossible. For example, they state neither homosexuals nor heterosexuals ever change into the other orientation.

I disagree. I base this on a personal incident. I am a heterosexual. However, I recall that on one occasion in a store in Lexington, Kentucky, I saw an attractive female and looked the individual in the eye. Then I averted my glance and focused on a male and felt attracted to that person.

It was as if I was for a moment seeing the male person through that female individual's eyes. This example indicates to me that individuals can transform from heterosexual to homosexual and vice versa.

By the way, I know some persons who claim that sexual love (homosexual or heterosexual) is the most wonderful thing they have ever experienced. But these people often seem to indicate that they are only happy when engaged in such sexual love.

Although I am single and celibate, I am confident that for most of the 168 hours in a week I am happier than they are. The joy of true love is far better and more lasting than sexual love. I confess that I am a heterosexual male who does feel sexual lust at times, but I credit God for enabling me to control the lust.

Ideally, perhaps we would have no sexual lust at all. Instead of sexual love we would experience only Godlike love and friendship love.

Madalyn Murray O'Hair was arguably the most widely known atheist in United States history. I certainly considered it unusual when I heard her say "Thank God" following a speech she gave at the university I was attending back in 1979.

When Madalyn Murray O'Hair spoke in the University of Kentucky Student Center Ballroom in Lexington, Kentucky, on Sunday, March 4, 1979, I was still an agnostic. But I was open-minded and seriously considering both atheism and Christianity. Perhaps I was also considering other religions to some extent. However, atheism and Christianity interested me most, besides agnosticism.

I enjoyed attending seminars and lectures on various topics, but this one especially interested me. After hearing an impressive introduction of Madalyn Murray O'Hair, I listened attentively to her speech. I felt sure a person with so much formal education would present a clear, logical explanation for how she knew there was no God.

Her speech disappointed me. During her speech I didn't think she provided a convincing reason for being an atheist. She offered no conclusive proof that there was no God.

At the end of the Q&A session I sought to move toward the front to see if I could overhear Ms. O'Hair explaining/discussing how she knew there was no God. It was a large crowd, and it took quite a while for me to work my way to the front from my position near the back. But I saw a person I recognized as being the leader of the University of Kentucky's student atheist chapter moving toward the front. She was just a short distance in front of me. The crowd parted to make room for her progression toward the front (after she announced her title as head of UK's student atheist chapter), and I followed close behind her.

After I got to the front I listened to Ms. O'Hair converse informally with people. I didn't hear a conversation about how she knew there was no God.

But, I thought she might say something to that person as she was leaving. So, as she exited, I moved straight across the room, which was now somewhat less crowded, and waited as Ms. O'Hair approached the area where I was, near the exit Ms. O'Hair was moving toward. As she approached me, she looked at me and seemed undecided, perhaps nervous. I read her lips or overheard as she expressed concerns to her security detail about me being there on that side of the auditorium—after her having seen me a few minutes earlier near the front. There were some uniformed officers with her (state, city, or university police, I guess, but I don't remember which), in addition to her own accompaniment detail, and likely she perceived peaceful me as a potential threat. She had received numerous threats from various persons over the years due to her beliefs (or lack of beliefs) and her activities in support of atheism.

Then she commented to those with her that she thought that I was her friend, and as she approached me she was going to drop her purse. She told them not to pick it up and that she thought no one else in the crowd would either, unless I did. She added that if I picked it up and handed it to her she was going to thank me. If I didn't pick it up, she was going to pick it up herself, quickly look at it as if to ensure everything was there, say "Thank God" loudly, then she and the security detail would quickly leave.

As she neared me, she did just that. She dropped her purse, picked it up, said "Thank God" loudly, then she and the security detail left quickly.

I found that interesting. Some readers may be interested in reading a lengthier version of this story that is in my first book *True Christianity: It May Not Be What You Think*.

Chapter 8: Neighbor Apparently Thinking My Mom Could Change Into a Cat

The idea that a human being can change into some other creature (such as a cat) then change back into a human being seems farfetched. I am not claiming this happens, although I would not 100% rule out the possibility. I believe that almost anything is possible.

I remember vividly that when I was a boy in the mid-1960s in southeastern Kentucky, my sister on at least two occasions had a cat that died. My mom stated that she thought a neighbor was killing them because the neighbor thought my mom was a witch who changed into a cat and that by killing the cat she could stop the witchcraft.

You may find that hard to believe, but it is the truth, if my memory is accurate. By the way, I never saw my mom change into a cat.

Human metamorphosis may not occur, but often things that are rumored, spoken about, written about, or covered in science fiction stories have a significant amount of truth to them. So, who knows? At any rate, I am confident that my mom believed that the neighbor felt mom was changing into a cat sometimes.

As science advances, maybe things we now think of as either "magic" or "witchcraft" (or dismiss as not really happening) will be explained scientifically. For example, currently science indicates that human flight is impossible, but some people believe that there are human witches with the ability to fly.

Before dismissing such human flight as impossible, please try to read the rest of this brief chapter with an open mind. Maybe human flight will someday be proven scientifically possible.

For example, if a person is very slender with little weight in their chest/stomach and has very strong arms, very strong legs, and develops the ability to move or "flap" both legs and both arms in the proper direction(s) fast enough, maybe someday a scientific study will indicate that such a person can fly. Such a view may not be any more ridiculous than the Wright Brothers' views when they began building their first aircraft.

At least one person claimed that my mother was a witch who could fly—and seemed to believe it.

Who knows? Maybe there really are human witches who can fly—though I've never seen a witch fly.

Hypnotism seems strange to me, almost like magic. As a child, I wondered if hypnotism really worked or was just an illusion. My doubts were greatly reduced during my teenage years when someone apparently hypnotized several other people in my presence.

Though I now know hypnotism works, I feel that it is generally better to avoid hypnotism. Let's live in the real world, rather than under a hypnotic spell.

However, hypnotism is widely used by many for various purposes.

I want to make it clear that I have never studied hypnotism and don't know how to hypnotize people myself, nor do I desire to learn how to. But I have witnessed others being hypnotized on at least a few occasions since that day when I was a teenager and apparently have been hypnotized myself at least a few times.

I will briefly mention four additional cases of hypnotism among those that I know about besides that time when I was a teenager. All four happened in Kentucky.

(1) During a morning worship service at a church, one of the ministers apparently briefly hypnotized the entire congregation except for himself, the pastor, and me.

(2) Once when I visited a different church, the minister apparently briefly hypnotized the entire

congregation except for himself and me. Some ministers in a few Christian denominations apparently use hypnotism regularly in their worship services.

(3) On another occasion, when I was in a meeting at a university, a few men there hypnotized some others in the meeting while the speaker told a personal story they apparently didn't want everyone to hear.

(4) Once when I was walking to a store on a cold winter day wearing a ski mask, I decided to take a shortcut. Normally I try to stay on sidewalks and avoid walking on others' private property. But it was very cold so I decided to take a shortcut and walk through a bank drive-through lane. As I walked down the drive-through lane of the bank, I heard voices apparently coming from two women tellers inside the bank. One apparently said "hit him." The other replied, "I did, but he's still coming." Then the first one said something like, "hit him again, as hard as you can." The next thing I knew, I was walking in another direction perhaps a hundred feet away. One of the women apparently hypnotized me briefly, altered my direction, then released me from the hypnotic spell.

I know of at least a few other incidents of hypnotism, but to save space (and to avoid disclosing personal information about individuals that could be embarrassing) I'll omit mentioning them.

Effects and Purposes of Hypnotism

Apparently one main purpose of hypnotism is for use as a defensive weapon. For example, I guess someone could hypnotize a potential attacker to stop them, as a nonviolent form of self-defense, as the bank tellers may have been doing to me, possibly thinking I might be a threat to them, or perhaps they were just afraid I'd be struck by a bank customer's car as I walked through the drive-through lane. But presumably such uses of hypnotism could be dangerous. If I had been forced to walk in front of a car while hypnotized, perhaps it could have been fatal. However, I do think that after I was released from the hypnotic spell by the bank teller(s) that I heard them discuss the possibility of my being hit by a car, and one of them said she was watching for cars as I was walking under the hypnotic spell.

Maybe Jesus used hypnotism as a defensive weapon in the situation described in Luke 4:28–30. But that is just speculation since scripture doesn't say. My opinion is that God has better powers than hypnotism for his true followers to use.

Hypnotism can also be used to alter behavior—for better or worse—by planting thoughts or instructions into a person's mind while they are under hypnosis. Also, memory apparently can be altered during hypnotism. Some memories apparently can be removed and false memories planted into the mind. And in cases where the hypnotized subjects are rendered physically immobile for a period of time, subjects apparently have no memory of events that occurred while they were hypnotized. Hypnotism alters persons' perceptions of reality.

Catholic priests, some other ministers, and others seem to use hypnotism as a tool to prevent part of church congregations (and other groups or individuals) from hearing something they are telling others. I believe many store employees also use something similar to hypnotism to refocus customers' eyes toward objects they want them to purchase. Similarly, some women seem to deliberately focus men's eyes as a way to flirt and to test a man's interest in them. I know personally there have been times that my eyes were refocused for some reason to areas I was not interested in looking at. I simply refocused my eyes in what I considered the proper direction, and I feel no harm was done. But I think hypnotism can potentially cause unnecessary purchases in a store and inappropriate romantic relationships between persons, among other harmful effects.

However, in many cases hypnotism is likely used constructively to help people. For example, some medical professionals use hypnotism as one tool to help persons with various problems. Still, even medical professionals probably misuse hypnotism (deliberately or inadvertently) in at least some cases. For example, there are apparently cases of false memories being planted in people while they were under hypnosis by a medical professional.

Closing Thoughts on Hypnotism

I am not a medical professional, so I can't give any medical advice. However, I believe that there are better ways of handling most (if not all) situations than by resorting to hypnotism. I feel hypnotism can be very dangerous if abused and is unnecessary in most, if not all, cases. But I confess that my knowledge about it is very limited compared to that of those who have studied it extensively and practice it professionally. As I stated earlier, I do not know how to hypnotize people and don't desire to learn how to do so.

I hope this chapter succeeded in alerting readers to the facts that hypnotism works and that it can be dangerous if used by amateurs or abused by well-trained professionals. If any of you are hypnotists, please use hypnotism responsibly or not at all.

Chapter 11: U.S. Government Mind-Control Experiments

In the past the United States government (and others) conducted mind-control experiments. Sometimes the experiments involved mind-altering drugs like LSD. These experiments likely contributed to at least some mental disorders suffered by various persons. Fortunately, I was never subjected to any mind-altering drugs by the government—at least as far as I know.

You can read more in numerous sources about the United States government "Project MKULTRA" mind-control experiments that sometimes involved the use of LSD on unsuspecting people. These sources include the three pieces whose URLs are located at the end of this sentence, on the websites of the *New York Times* (https://www.nytimes.com/packages/pdf/national/13inmate_ProjectMKULTRA.pdf), the *Los Angeles Times* (https://latimes.com/archives/la-xpm-1999-apr-04-me-24126-story.html), and *Time* (http://content.time.com/time/specials/packages/article/0,28804,2008962_2008964_2008992,00.html).

I don't know if I was ever part of a government experiment or not. But some of the unusual things I've experienced make me wonder if I was part of Project MKULTRA as a child.

My understanding is that some of the experiments involved young children. I may write more about the United States government mind control experiments at some time in the future, including more details about why I feel that I may have been an involuntary participant in such experiments.

Chapter 12: A Person Altering the Dreams of Another Individual Who Is Asleep

One individual can transmit thoughts into a second individual's dreams while the second individual is sleeping, thus altering those dreams. I believe this based on some personal experiences that I may elaborate more about at some time in the future in another book (or an article).

But for persons seeking scientific evidence, I suggest you consider going to a good research library and accessing a journal article from some decades ago titled "An Experimental Approach to Dreams and Telepathy: II. Report of Three Studies" in the March 1970 issue of the *American Journal of Psychiatry*. That article discussed a scientific study by Montague Ullman, M.D., and Stanley Krippner, Ph.D., regarding this topic. I first read about the study on page 254 of M. Scott Peck's 1978 book, *The Road Less Traveled* (published by the Touchstone imprint of Simon & Schuster), then went to the University of Kentucky Medical Center Library and found the actual journal article. The article amazed me. I encourage you to consider reading at least part of it.

As I stated earlier, I feel that on at least a few occasions others have transmitted thoughts to me to alter my dreams, but a scientific study hasn't been done on me, so you'll just have to accept (or not accept) my opinion.

I will end this brief discussion about dreams by stating that I feel strongly that it is important that no one ever alter anyone's dreams in an effort to do harm.

During a visit to Washington, D.C., several years ago, as I rode an escalator up from the subway to street level, several persons in a hurry were walking quickly up past me while I stood stationary on the moving escalator. I thought they were being rude, and looked them in the eye indicating it. Someone below me said something like "he better watch it, or someone will hit him." I kept doing it, then suddenly when I looked at one person, I felt a brief sharp eye pain. I got the impression that the eye pain was to cue me that people considered it rude to look at people as I was doing rather than standing on the right side of the escalator step to politely let people pass me on the left.

After this, as I looked down at the bottom of the escalator, I noticed that there were several people lining up to get on, so it seemed to be rush hour. However, I would have preferred someone simply tell me it was rush hour and a long line was developing at the bottom of the escalator, so please move to the right to let people pass— rather than give me the brief eye pain. I could have even walked up the escalator myself instead of riding passively had I known. I probably should have been more observant.

I also felt a similar brief sharp eye pain on at least one other occasion, also several years ago, here in Kentucky; I discussed that incident briefly earlier, in chapter 4, titled "Example of 'Miraculous Healing.' "

Is there a logical reason for this eye pain? Do certain people have the power to cause it? Maybe I should pray about what to do as soon as I hear a voice saying something about "hit him."

On several occasions in the 1990s (and on a few occasions since), I experienced a brief sharp chest pain. I got the impression that the pain was caused by certain persons looking at me and focusing their eyes and/or thoughts on me in some particular way to deliberately cause it. Below I describe one specific instance.

Once I experienced the brief chest pain during a visit to New York City. I was walking on the Brooklyn Heights Promenade and saw some benches. I noticed that they were all empty and sat down on one to enjoy the view. After a few minutes, I thought I ought to get up so others could sit down; surprisingly, I saw that the other benches were all still empty, despite the large number of people in the area. I wondered why. I saw no sign saying people could not sit on the benches, nor did I see a sign limiting how long one could sit on them. I felt that somehow they were deliberately kept empty.

I prayed about how the benches were kept empty. Then I felt a brief sharp pain in my chest, and an inaudible voice stated "that's how we do it." I can understand the need to have a method of keeping persons from monopolizing the benches, but I hope there is a better way to do it than causing a brief sharp chest pain.

My guess is that some people apparently have the power to cause others to experience chest pains, perhaps as a way to control their behavior. I wonder if this could be the cause of some heart attacks?

The few people I mentioned the brief chest pains to stated that they were my imagination. However, the pains certainly felt real, though they only lasted a second or a fraction of a second each.

Thankfully, I haven't felt any recently, but what caused these brief pains? What can or should be done to prevent me or anyone else from experiencing them? If they are a method of controlling behavior, I like to think that there is a better one.

Chapter 15: My Paternal Grandmother's Funeral: Did She Move Her Eyes?

I attended my paternal grandmother Irene Depew-Gibson's funeral in Floyd County, Kentucky, when I was five years old. It is one of my earliest memories. Perhaps one reason I remember it so well is that on the drive to it mom repeatedly told me how important it was for me to behave, stating that my grandmother would be up front in a casket, but I couldn't go up to her. Another reason I remember it so well is something very unusual that happened as I looked at my grandmother in her casket.

When we got to the funeral, the casket was in the back of the room, and so I asked mom if I could walk over and look at it. I think she asked dad if it was okay and he agreed it was. So I did. As I looked at my grandmother in the casket, I saw her eyes "sparkle" and move a few times. I told mom at least a few times that I thought my grandmother was alive.

I even thought I heard my grandmother ask me to climb up into the casket. I thought I heard her say that at least a couple more times, so I started to do so. I thought obeying her voice might revive her and make her happy. Then mom came over and got me before I could climb up. As I turned around, I saw the man up front had stopped speaking and several people had turned around to look at the back where we were. I think we had arrived late and though my Auntie Alice, dad's sister Alice Gibson-Martin, came back to say she'd saved seats up front for us, dad said we'd stay in the back. I asked if the service was over, and I think mom said no. I asked why the man had stopped talking and people were turned around in their seats looking back, and mom said I had created a scene that interrupted. I guess I did.

On at least a few occasions there at the funeral I had thought I saw my grandmother's eyes move, thought she was alive, and even thought she was talking to me. After I told mom about the eyes moving and begged her to look, she walked over to look to appease me. Mom was looking once as my grandmother's eyes moved. After that, I heard mom tell dad that she thought she saw his mom's eyes move, too; she asked him to look, but he didn't. He thought it was crazy, and even at age five I could understand why. By the way, mom didn't remember this incident when I described it to her years later. Was I a five-year-old having an illusion? Is my memory faulty?

During part of the mid1980s I worked for the U.S. Postal Service in Lexington, Kentucky, at the Nandino Boulevard mail sorting facility. We workers typically dressed in casual clothes since we worked in the back where we were typically out of public sight. Though we wore casual clothes, on a few nights several persons in dress clothes wearing ties showed up and began walking laps around the mail sorting facility.

I asked some other workers who these strangers were and why they were there, but the workers I asked didn't seem to know. Then one night as this group of well-dressed persons walked past the area where I worked, another worker asked one of them something like, "When are those people supposed to be killed at that Post Office in Oklahoma?" The other person replied something like, "How do you know about that? Nobody is supposed to know about it. If people know about it, it won't happen." After a very brief hesitation, he added, "Maybe it shouldn't happen."

The worker and the other person also exchanged a few other comments. I don't remember their exact words and may not have heard them all originally. But, among the comments, I think the other person said something about the worker picking me to overhear the conversation. I got the impression that they had planned in advance to have a conversation on this subject and at least one of them wanted another person to overhear. The person who had been walking laps with the group said something like "I don't trust all these persons I'm walking with, though I do most of them and they were carefully selected for this." This indicated to me that the persons chosen to walk laps around the facility were carefully selected.

Was this a joke? Did someone tell my coworker to ask that question? I don't know. He asked the question loudly enough that at least a few of the persons in dress clothes presumably heard it in addition to the one who answered him. A specific date or a specific location in Oklahoma wasn't mentioned, but I don't think it was very many days after that when several persons were killed at a U.S. Postal Service facility in Edmond, Oklahoma, apparently by a crazed individual.

I wonder if this was a planned thing or a coincidence. Could it have been some type of government mind control experiment? Did someone tell my coworker to ask that question? Why were those persons in dress clothes all walking laps around the building? Did my thinking about it somehow make what happened in Oklahoma happen? I was scared after the tragedy in Oklahoma occurred and wanted to talk to my coworker to ask him about the question he asked, but he was absent for quite a while afterward and the coworkers I asked said they didn't know where he was at. I thought I heard one of them whisper that he was psychiatrically hospitalized, but I'm not sure.

No one ever spoke to me about the specific details of that conversation again, and I was apparently followed around by several people for at least a few years and received what I interpreted as a few veiled death threats. When I tried to approach one of those following me, he retreated.

Out of fear, I didn't speak to anyone or write anyone about the incident until years later. The few people I've spoken to about the incident seemed to not take it seriously or to have been scared. One specifically told me to never speak about it again, and said he had orders to kill me if I did.

For some reason, I did not ask the coworker who asked that question about Oklahoma why he asked it, when he did return to work. For one thing, I think we typically worked in different areas then. Also, due to my being a temporary worker at the time I heard the conversation, I wasn't there long afterward myself, though I was called back to work later. When I finally did happen to see him there, as he walked up to me, he instructed me not to "say anything about the thing we both know because we are being watched," or words similar to that. I interpreted this to mean that as we talked, we were being watched to see what we spoke about since this was the first time the two of us had been together since the Oklahoma shootings.

Years later, long after I had left my work for the Postal Service, when I finally phoned my former coworker who had asked the question and described to him my memory of the conversation, he said he didn't remember it. One possible reason for his apparent memory lapse is the fact that when I spoke to him on the phone, speaking extemporaneously, my description of the conversation I had overheard about Oklahoma was not completely accurate, due to my inadvertently misspeaking. Another possibility is fear; he may have gotten threats as I did. I know I had plenty of fear after the Oklahoma shootings, due to what I perceived as veiled threats, due to the people following me around that didn't speak to me and retreated from me when I approached them, and due to some other unusual occurrences soon afterward. If all those people in the dress clothes circling around our Postal Service facility knew what happened, I wondered why nothing was reported in the media about it.

I waited years to write about this. Initially my hesitation was due to fear, then later when I prayed about it, I felt that the time was not yet right to write about it— until recent years. I would love to elaborate a bit more on what I went through during the period after the Oklahoma shootings as a result of them and the conversation I overheard, but I feel that it would do more harm than good at this time.

It is possible that my memory is faulty, but I believe that this account written here is accurate. Memories can be faulty, however, and the conversation I remember overhearing (as well as the tragedy in Oklahoma) took place over 30 years ago (in 1986).

On several occasions, I have apparently heard persons talking who were far away from me and/or perhaps read the thoughts of persons who were far away from me. I was too far away to hear them or to read their lips in my opinion. Also, on various occasions, others seem to have read my thoughts, based on their reactions.

The first occasion that I remember hearing a conversation from relatively far away was when I was a young boy in about the first grade on a trip with my dad, paternal grandfather, and a couple of other people to visit my grandfather's brother and his wife in eastern Virginia. On a visit to a shipyard during that trip, a visit that only dad, my grandfather, and I took, I heard the voices of a couple talking; they were several feet away. My grandfather said to my dad that he heard those persons' voices through me and stated something like "the boy has the hearing; maybe someone will teach him to talk when he gets older; maybe everyone can hear; maybe everyone can talk. We don't know much about how it works." My grandfather seemed to be referring to how people can hear voices from far away and speak in a voice that can be heard far away.

On some of the occasions that I hear these voices, if someone else is near me, sometimes the individual near me will touch one of their ears with a finger. Perhaps they are indicating they are hearing the same voice? Or, perhaps it is coincidence or a reaction to some mannerism of mine. The times I've asked, the person touching their ear didn't indicate hearing anything.

How does this super hearing or extra loud talking work? I feel it is a gift of God to be used for good.

I feel it is very important for us to help preserve the wonderful planet God has provided. It would be a shame if wonders like the Grand Canyon, Great Smoky Mountains, Yellowstone, Yosemite, or other priceless natural treasures were irreparably damaged or destroyed.

The awesome diversity of our planet is an astounding testament to God, as I see it. Plants, animals, mountains, valleys, lakes, rivers, oceans, deserts, etc., illustrate that. I want to discuss one of those features, a magnificent cave in Kentucky—and not Mammoth Cave.

Here in Kentucky, numerous beautiful caves are one of the unusual features that add magnificent diversity to the area. Mammoth Cave is the best known one, famous for its spectacular beauty and for being the longest known cavern in the world. But among Kentucky's many caves is a second huge cave along the Kentucky-Virginia border. By the way, since the cavern borders the two states, I'm not sure how much of it is in Kentucky and how much is in Virginia.

Huge Cave Along the Kentucky-Virginia Border

The cave helps indicate the awesome beauty and diversity of God's creation. It currently gets little attention, although it could be the world's second longest cave—its fabulous beauty rivaling Mammoth Cave's.

I'll preface my comments about it by urging readers not to rush down to see it due to the danger (as well as the risk of doing priceless damage to parts of the cavern and/or bats living in it). If you choose to visit anyway, please get permission from property owners, make sure you are well trained and equipped properly, tell a friend exactly where you are entering and when you will be exiting, and be very cautious. Caving can be extremely dangerous due to slippery surfaces, sudden drop-offs, overhanging rocks, flash flooding from unexpected rainfalls, and of course the risk of getting lost in a huge cave with numerous passages, in addition to other factors, including lack of oxygen in some cases. Please prepare carefully and thoroughly. Be aware also of federal and state laws that exist to protect caves and artifacts inside them.

My dad enjoyed reading an article I wrote similar to this chapter's contents about two months before he passed on to heaven (at age 82) on April 27, 2013. I told him I planned to include a chapter in my book about the cave. I did include a chapter about the cave in my first book, *True Christianity: It May Not Be What You Think*, which I was writing at the time. I self-published it in 2014 (second edition 2015, third edition 2017), and this chapter is similar to that chapter.

Personally, I only went caving a few times with dad because of the dangers involved. I haven't been in a cave in decades. But if/when parts of this huge cave are opened for tours, I would love to take a tour and see the river, the cave's magnificent colors, and some other marvelous sights I haven't seen personally—if I am still alive and fit enough to do so at that time. However, I urge readers desiring to tour a huge Kentucky cave soon to take one or more of the scheduled tours of Mammoth Cave in western Kentucky instead of entering this one. By the way, just as only a small part of Mammoth Cave is open to tours, at most I think only a small part of this huge cave along the Kentucky-Virginia border will ever be opened to tours.

Explorations by the Author's Dad

This author's dad, William E. "Bill" Gibson, over a few decades explored parts of the cavern in his spare time. Dad told of its magnificent beauty to me and many others numerous times over the years, before he passed on to heaven. He described various beautiful colors that he said his pictures did not do justice to, huge rooms, numerous stalactites and stalagmites—and a big river flowing through one level of it.

I think dad's explorations began as a search for silver mines allegedly operated by John Swift in the 18th century in Kentucky. But dad also enjoyed being outdoors, hiking, and caving. Though he never found a silver mine, dad said he did find some silver coins.

Dad called the cave "The Cavern of the Shawnees." He said several times that it extends at least from the Breaks area near Elkhorn City, Kentucky to the Cumberland Gap and Middlesboro area. This is a distance of more than 75 miles. And in one phone conversation he told me that it may begin before the Breaks and end past Middlesboro.

Dad told me the cave contains passages on multiple vertical levels. He added that numerous entrances lead into the cave.

If all the passages are mapped, this author believes that the total length of them could be a couple hundred miles, making it the world's second longest known cave.

Shawnee Indian Knowledge of the Cave

Though it lacks fame today, the cave apparently was well known centuries ago. The Shawnee Indians knew about the cave, according to the five volume 1922 *History of Kentucky*, which states Charles Blue-Jacket described the cave as "many miles in extent."

The book notes "that it could be entered at several different points and on both sides of the great mountain range." The book also states that "To the hoof-beats of the horse along the roadway through Pound Gap the mountain sounds . . . hollow, especially when the solid rock is trodden." (This five volume book was edited by Judge Charles Kerr, copyright 1922 by The American Historical Society, and discusses the cave on pages 128 and 129 of Volume I, in a chapter written by William Elsey Connelley.)

My dad informed me that one part of the cave is very sacred to the Shawnee Indians. Dad told me either that he was told or that he read (I'm not sure which) "that no white man will ever enter" that part of the cave. That may be true, and I think it is very important to try to take reasonable steps to protect the entire cave from abuse and damage.

Explorations by Ray Love and Articles That Followed

Ray Love, after exploring parts of the cave, in 1971 provided an awesome description, reported by Kenneth Paul Mink in the Hazard, Kentucky *Hazard Herald* newspaper in its April 30, 1971 issue. Numerous other news sources carried this impressive report via the Associated Press.

In May 1971 various publications provided more details about the cave, Ray Love's explorations, and the cave potentially becoming a major tourist attraction for the area. A nicely written article in the May 6, 1971 Louisville *Courier-Journal* by staff writer Kyle Vance cites spelunkers reporting finding "two 50-foot waterfalls, a river running 20 feet deep . . . and one chamber so high that misty clouds form at the ceiling" to quote Vance's words.

I urge persons to consider seeking to read the complete *Hazard Herald* and Louisville *Courier-Journal* articles I referenced.

Recent Years and the Future

As far as I know, the media has written little about the cave in recent decades. It certainly has not become a major tourist attraction.

Furthermore, I am concerned that damage possibly occurred to parts of the cave during construction of a four-lane road some years ago over the mountain between Jenkins, Kentucky, and Virginia. Also, quarrying operations in various locations along the many miles of the area where the cave exists potentially can damage it—if they haven't already. Additionally, irresponsible spelunkers may damage it and steal items for their personal collections, as some probably have.

Much of the cave is on private property. This can be good or bad depending on how property owners care for it. Somehow the cave needs protected from those who would abuse it. Also, keeping numerous cave entrances open is important for ventilation and for easy access to the lengthy cave. Unfortunately, several entrances have already been sealed.

The ongoing formation of the Pine Mountain State Scenic Trail, a linear state park that basically follows the area of the cave, may help protect this underground marvel. But that remains to be seen.

Cave Is a Priceless Treasure of Unknown Size

This cave seems to be a priceless treasure. Its natural beauty is beyond value, and items possibly left in it by Indians, early settlers, etc., make it even more magnificent. Perhaps ancient peoples that preceded the Indians explored the cave and left priceless artifacts. It would be a terrible shame if vandals damaged or destroyed either these items or the cave itself, or if artifacts were permanently lost due to entrances being sealed up—as many entrances already have been.

Only God knows the total size of the cavern. I doubt any human has explored more than a small part of it. Reasons for this include limitations on the length of time lights last, as well as the need to carry adequate rope, food, and other items underground. Also, many entrances are small, which discourages some explorers.

Descriptions provided by my dad, Ray Love, Blue-Jacket, and others indicate the cave is a magnificent wonder of nature. It would be marvelous if more actions are taken to preserve this priceless treasure for future generations. Perhaps at least parts of it can be developed as a tourist attraction, too.

Let's seek to protect this priceless underground marvel and all the other priceless creations God has provided, when reasonably possible. I consider this part of true Christianity, seeking to do God's perfect will.

For those who haven't heard of the Philadelphia Experiment, I will offer a brief two sentence summary. During the 1940s the United States Navy allegedly (The Navy denies it.) conducted experiments on invisibility that enabled a ship and its crew to basically become invisible. Supposedly, in one of the experiments, a ship in Philadelphia apparently not only became invisible but was transported to Norfolk, Virginia, and back within minutes.

You may read more about what supposedly happened during the experiment in various online articles. You may also read the book *The Philadelphia Experiment: Project Invisibility* (copyright 1979) by William L. Moore and Charles Berlitz.

My main reason for including a chapter in this book about the Philadelphia Experiment is a trip that I took with my dad, my paternal grandfather, an uncle, and another relative to visit my grandfather's brother, Charles "Guy" Gibson, who had served in the United States Navy.

My dad said he thought Guy was a welder on Navy ships. At any rate, Guy was a career U.S. Navy person. I think he was retired and living in Newport News, Virginia at the time of our visit in the mid1960s when I was probably about six or seven years old.

During our visit, my dad and/or my grandfather asked Guy about that experiment. Even at my age I was astounded by what the adults discussed. I remember hearing them talk about a ship disappearing and reappearing and Guy talking about a letter he received from Albert Einstein. Einstein may have headed up the experiment, but even if he didn't, he was apparently involved with it or at least aware of it. Guy said that the letter from Einstein alluded to the experiment, but did not specifically mention it. He said Einstein sent that letter to many people. He said Einstein wanted as many people as possible to know about it to try to stop the experiment, which he felt was doing more harm than good.

My grandfather's brother also mentioned a more detailed, specific letter that some people got from Einstein about the experiment. He said he did not get a copy of that letter, but he either heard about it or saw it— I'm not sure which. Guy made it clear that he was not involved in the experiment, but that he knew enough about it from enough people to know it had occurred. Furthermore, various problems came from the experiment, including major negative health effects on many of the participants. I believe some people even died.

I firmly believe that the Philadelphia Experiment happened, but I admit that I lack any proof for it. The hearsay evidence from Guy that I overheard certainly wouldn't be convincing proof, especially coming from my memories as a boy either in the first grade or having just completed the first grade (me, at the time I visited him).

But the numerous articles, etc., that in some cases include reports from eyewitnesses and/or participants might help convince those with open minds. Google "Philadelphia Experiment" and see what you find. As an alternative, seek to buy or check out from a library the book I mentioned earlier.

Remember that if something seems to be scientifically impossible, it is possible that the event illustrates the limitations of science. Scientists are not perfect, and they lack knowledge about many things. Also, scientists sometimes keep certain things secret for various reasons. Yes, I believe sometimes truth can seem stranger than fiction, and the Philadelphia Experiment is an example, as I see it.

My paternal grandmother's brother, George Depew, devoted his career to service for the United States Navy. My dad told me that George had been involved in some top secret research that George could not discuss with his family.

But, according to George Depew's son (also named George Depew), the United States Air Force Museum in Dayton, Ohio, used to have a large picture of George Depew with the caption "Father of radar" on it. Apparently, one of the secret projects he worked on was radar.

The United States Navy facilities in Hawaii were one of the first places that radar was installed. According to one story I was told, George Depew personally trained the personnel in Hawaii on how to use the radar and how to distinguish birds from enemy aircraft on the newly installed radar.

According to the story, supposedly, on the morning of December 7, 1941, when a person at the radar saw a huge number of what looked like enemy aircraft, he called his supervisor over. They assumed that they were birds. Someone phoned Washington, D.C., and told George Depew that a huge flock of birds on the radar looked like what he had described as enemy aircraft instead of what he had described as birds.

George Depew asked which direction the birds were flying, and they told him that they were flying toward the naval base. He instructed them to get a spotter up to see what type of birds they were and to take some photos when they got close, since these birds apparently didn't show up on radar like normal birds did. He then got off the phone, waited for them to phone back with a description of the birds, and plans were made for him to fly to Hawaii to help with the radar.

A few minutes later the return call came. The speaker on the phone stated that the objects on the radar were not birds, they were enemy aircraft in huge numbers, and the naval base was under attack. As you may remember from studying history, on December 7, 1941, the United States Naval Base at Pearl Harbor, Hawaii, was attacked by the Japanese.

I think the person who told the story to me said that George Depew joked that he practically got both court-marshaled and promoted on the same day.

It has been many years since this story was told to me, and I have no idea whether or not it is true. But the fact that George Depew did have a career with the Navy, did perform secret research, and at least some of this research involved radar lead me to believe that the story is basically true. But I don't remember who told the story to me, and I admit that I don't know if it is true.

Many years ago someone told a story that is supposedly true about an incident that happened during World War II. It has been many years since I heard the story, and the person who told it to me was repeating it from another source, so my summary below may not be exactly correct. But, to the best of my memory, the account following this paragraph is accurate.

According to the story, during World War II, when one particular teenage boy in southeastern Kentucky did not show up in response to being drafted to fight in the war, a couple of government officials went to his home to find out the reason.

The two officials drove up the hollow where the boy lived. It was a very hot summer day with the temperature at least in the 90s Fahrenheit.

When the men reached the boy's home, almost as soon as they got out of the car they were met by the boy's mother. She asked them why they were there.

They verified the address, and then said they were there because her son had not responded to his draft notice. The mother told them that she and her family loved everyone including the Germans, and that her son was not going to go to war to fight.

They asked if her family members were conscientious objectors, and the mom replied no, we just love everyone and are opposed to war. Then she urged

59

the officials to leave before the snow came. They laughed, and said it would be months before it snowed.

The mother said something like, "No, it won't. I feel a big snow coming on right now. You better leave quickly." They laughed again, and one said something like "It's over 90 degrees here; it can't snow."

Then the wind began to blow hard, and the temperature began to drop. Then snowflakes began to fall. Then it began to snow harder. According to the story, the men left and never came back.

You may find this story especially hard to believe. And it does seem farfetched. But I feel that even the weather can be controlled by strong prayers of a righteous person in some spiritual way that I don't understand. The Bible in James 5:16 states ". . . . The effectual fervent prayer of a righteous man availeth much." (KJV)

And this lady in the story certainly seemed righteous due to her commitment to love everyone. She seemed to be following Jesus' instructions to love even one's enemies. She certainly didn't desire to fight the Germans. And it is perhaps important to remember that during World War II many of the German soldiers were Christians, at least members of Christian churches, and wore belt buckles with the approximate English equivalent of "God with us" on them.

Often both sides in wars contain huge numbers of soldiers who claim to be Christians with God on their side. This lady may have had the right idea.

I know of at least two occasions when objects rose and fell without being touched, apparently due to a human using some type of invisible force.

End Table Being Elevated and Lowered

The first occasion involved a wooden end table. I walked into my dad and mom's living room in Jenkins, Kentucky, one day as an end table lowered to the floor. I asked dad what caused it. He said something like "he raised and lowered it," pointing to another gentleman who was there.

Apparently, through some way of focusing his mind, that man had somehow managed to elevate an end table in dad and mom's living room, then lower it back down, without touching it with any object in any way.

Some years later dad told me the man had stopped doing such things. Dad also said that the man told him that Native American Indians taught him how to do the levitating and the lowering of objects. Dad said that the man told him that it was the devil or evil forces who gave such power, and that he didn't do such things anymore; the man was a Christian now.

Knife Rising and Moving Around, Lowering Again

Another occurrence of an object rising and lowering occurred one day in my apartment when I lived in Nicholasville, Kentucky.

A knife that was lying on a counter in my kitchen suddenly rose up in the air and moved around the area near the counter briefly.

Then I heard an inaudible voice that sounded like my apartment manager (a nice senior citizen who lived in the apartment below me) say something like, "I better let that knife down. I don't know where he's standing, and I don't want to hurt him. I just did it to show him how such things can happen to warn him if/when he moves back to southeastern Kentucky to be with his parents."

In theory, I guess she could have had a powerful magnet down below that she moved around to cause the knife to rise up and to lower. As most readers may know, a magnet will attract metal objects or repel them depending on which pole of the magnet is pointed toward the object.

But I am convinced that she did not use a magnet. She was a woman of strong faith who (in my opinion) used spiritual power to cause this to happen.

Final Thoughts on Elevating Objects

I am convinced that objects can be elevated and lowered through methods that scientists can't explain.

But I urge readers not to try such things due to the risks. In fact, in both incidents described in this chapter, the persons stopped. In the first case, the man has completely stopped doing such things—he decided it was wrong. The second person stopped moving the knife out of fear for my safety.

It is amazing to me that a person can use a stick or a piece of metal to find water. But, apparently there are some persons who are gifted to be able to find water using nothing more than a stick or a piece of metal shaped a certain way.

This is called dowsing for water. I have never done it, and I have never seen it done. But I firmly believe that it can be done, therefore I am including this subject in my book about true stories that may seem stranger than fiction.

My dad told me about witnessing someone dowsing for water, seeing the stick dip toward the ground in the presence of water. This skill for finding water may be very helpful for persons living in drought-stricken areas who need to find a location to drill for a well, etc.

If you don't believe in dowsing, I urge you to do an Internet search for "dowsing for water." (You don't need to put dowsing for water in quotes in your search.) Then, read with an open mind some of the numerous online articles on the subject.

I am confident that the highest righteous authority, which I call God, gifts us with enormous powers that we often don't understand or use properly. Yes, sometimes truth can seem stranger than fiction.

Chapter 24: Buying and Reading the *Los Angeles Times* in New York City

Perhaps this story is not as strange as some of the others in this book, but I found it interesting. Perhaps you will, too. On a visit to New York City, about 20 years ago, I was interested in reading about the news in other areas. I bought copies of various New York City newspapers and skimmed through them.

I was surprised at how little news these newspapers contained from certain other areas. New York City is the largest city in the United States and very diverse, so I was expecting more diverse news coverage.

But New York City is an island, and perhaps in some way its residents become so focused on New York City and areas that impact it that certain other news events do not get covered.

At any rate, on that particular day I went to a news stand and bought a copy of the *Los Angeles Times* to get some news coverage that was not in the New York papers. The New York papers had much coverage that wasn't in the *Los Angeles Times*, but the reverse was also certainly true.

Wherever you are, I urge you to try to seek news coverage from a source outside of your area, and with the Internet that is easier now than when I took that trip to New York City.

One interesting fact is that when I bought the *Los Angeles Times* that day, the gentleman who sold it to me mentioned his name and asked me to tell Tom Brokaw who was then the news anchor on NBC's evening newscast that he said hi. I didn't know what he meant.

But, as I sat down and began reading the paper, I heard the man tell a coworker that I must have been buying that paper for myself. He said he had thought I was buying it for Tom Brokaw because he was normally the only one who bought the *Los Angeles Times* from that newsstand that early in the morning. He said sometimes Mr. Brokaw bought it himself, but usually someone else came down and got it for him, adding that Mr. Brokaw or someone acting on his behalf apparently didn't buy it every day, at least from this news stand, but frequently did.

He then added that I was apparently reading it for the same reason Mr. Brokaw did. I felt honored to be compared to Mr. Brokaw. I do want to make it clear though that this was the only day I skimmed the *Los Angeles Times* that way.

I hope you enjoyed reading this story and didn't find it a sidetrack from the topic of the book. I will close this chapter by urging persons to seek multiple news sources when they want facts and to read with an open mind. And of course, if the multiple sources all cite the same original source, it's perhaps good sometimes to think of it as only being one source.

My dad devoted several years of his life to a part-time search for silver mines allegedly operated in southeastern Kentucky by John Swift in the 1700s. Dad stated that he never found a mine, but that he did find some silver coins.

As a boy, I enjoyed hiking in the Red River Gorge area, Breaks Interstate Park area, and the Jenkins, Kentucky area with dad during his search. My interest was primarily in the hiking, beautiful rock formations and other natural beauty, etc., and we never found any silver on my trips with him. But I am confident that silver coins and maybe one or more silver mines do exist in eastern Kentucky.

The area of the Pine Mountain fault in the Jenkins, Kentucky, area may be a prime location for one or more silver mines. But, since many persons have looked for the mines over the years (apparently unsuccessfully), I am confident that if the mines exist, their entrances have been sealed (as Swift mentioned sealing them in his journal), and/or persons who know about them are keeping them secret.

Obviously, for one to legally mine silver, one must own the property or at least the mineral rights, so I urge readers not to rush down to southeastern Kentucky (as so many have in the past) and spend much time and money on a search that might involve trespassing on others' property and doing irreparable damage to priceless natural wonders in a fruitless search for a silver mine that (1) may not exist, (2) may be owned by someone else who has the right to keep it secret, or (3) may be so well concealed that one would have no success finding it, etc.

For what it's worth, I do believe that silver in some form is or was in southeastern Kentucky. But, even if it is/was a great silver mine, I think the value of any silver that is/was in it pales in comparison to the priceless natural beauty of the area, including the magnificence of a large cave in the area that I discussed in Chapter 18.

One thing that many persons in the United States pride ourselves on is what we often call "freedom of the press." And in the United States we do have more freedom in this regard than exists in many (most?) other parts of the world. However, our freedom has limits.

This chapter focuses on freedom of the press with regard to an incident during the Vietnam War. During that period, there were many protests against the war by military veterans, college students, etc. One of the most widely reported protests occurred at Kent State University where exhausted, armed National Guard troops opened fire, killing some students, including at least one innocent student who was not participating in the protests. You can read about the Kent State shootings in numerous articles available online and in print.

According to one source, after the Kent State shootings the government was deeply concerned about the potential negative effects of news coverage of this tragedy. Supposedly, government officials fanned out to seek to censor what was reported.

That night government officials descended upon one major newspaper in the region, thinking it might have had a reporter on the scene at the protest and perhaps thinking that it might be printing a story that would enrage public opinion, according to the same source mentioned in the previous paragraph.

68

That source stated that, as it turned out, the paper did not have a reporter there. The only story in the paper that was being printed for the next day was an Associated Press article that had already been vetted by the government.

The government officials just asked the paper's owner to stop the presses and change the newspaper headline for the article. At first the owner refused to even do this.

But, according to my source, some of the officials also went to the newspaper owner's home and spoke to the owner's wife. His wife and young daughter were very frightened, and his wife phoned her husband at the paper and urged him to do whatever these government men wanted, that she and her daughter were very frightened.

The newspaper owner then relented and changed the headline. I heard this story when I was in college from a source that I consider reputable, but I admit that it is only hearsay.

Even assuming the story is true, maybe it was right to censor the newspaper's headline. Government censors may have had the right idea. I don't know the original headline's wording. But I do think that it is important to realize that our freedom of the press in the United States is not total. Maybe more freedom is needed—or maybe not.

Either voluntarily or involuntarily, much of the news reported by major news outlets is either vetted by the government or provided by government sources.

Probably there are government agents from the National Security Agency or other secretive government agencies on the payroll at many major news outlets.

Apparently one of the largest governmental organizations is the National Security Agency, which may have thousands of persons who perhaps seek to spy on others and to control the flow of information in one way or another, and to use information for the government's own purposes.

Even in the Internet age, we lack total freedom. For example, the information on the Internet is only valuable if one knows how to access the right information and does so. Furthermore, certain countries limit Internet access.

Though I am not a computer expert, I believe that shutting down a few major servers could probably shut down much or all of the Internet worldwide. Furthermore, if some person or some organization controlled for selfish purposes how a few search engines (such as Google) access information and prevented searchers from accessing a specific site, that would limit access greatly.

For example, if someone writes an article and posts it on the Internet, but the only way it can be accessed is for someone to type in the exact URL for it, it would likely drastically limit the number of people that read it.

The media has a responsibility to present the truth and to do so in a responsible way, as I see it. And the government also has a responsibility to do so. It is important to have reasonable boundaries to prevent abuses by government, media, or individuals.

In general, I support freedom of the press. And I hope this chapter has helped persons think constructively about our so-called freedom of the press.

Chapter 27: Speaker Apparently Reads Speech by Former CIA Agent Claiming U.S. Encouraged Iraq to Attack Kuwait

Did the U.S. encourage the Iraqi invasion of Kuwait to create a crisis? A paper by former CIA agent Philip Agee titled "Producing the Proper Crisis" published in the November 1990 issue of *Z Magazine* indicates this.

And, a speaker at a free public lecture at the University of Kentucky that I attended read the paper, as reported in the *Kentucky Kernel*, UK's student newspaper on January 17, 1991. The event I attended took place (coincidentally?) the same evening that the U.S.-led attack against Iraq began. The speaker stated that the U.S. deliberately encouraged Saddam Hussein to attack Iraq. I urge readers to seek to read Agee's paper and some of his other writings on the Internet.

The public talk in the University of Kentucky Student Center had been scheduled well in advance, so it seems amazing (a coincidence?) that his talk was given the same evening the aerial bombardment began and was broadcast live on CNN. The next chapter (Chapter 28) discusses another "coincidence" involving the Iraq war.

Chapter 28: My Move to Nicholasville from Lexington the Same Day Hussein Invaded Kuwait (Coincidence?)

In 1990 I was planning to move from Lexington, Kentucky, to Nicholasville, Kentucky. Somehow I got the impression that if I moved from Lexington to Nicholasville I was going to be killed by the United States government. And I have received what I perceive to be death threats since my work for the U.S. Postal Service, and my overhearing a conversation there that I described in Chapter 16 of this book.

I prayed about my planned move to Nicholasville. Then I heard in answer to my prayer an inaudible inner voice urging me not to worry because the U.S. government would be concerned about more important things than me on that day.

So I moved on the day scheduled. And on the same day that I moved from Lexington to Nicholasville, Iraq invaded Kuwait.

By itself, this might just be a coincidence. But when taken along with all the other coincidences that I have experienced or witnessed in my life (including the one in the previous chapter about the Iraq war), I think more than coincidence is involved.

I remember an incident one day when I worked at a particular job at a location in Kentucky I won't disclose. It involved a customer in a car with a dog that came up to the drive-through window of the business. The dog appeared to be angry, barked ferociously, and seemed to try to jump out of the car. The drive-through window employee screamed, fearing that the dog would jump out of the car and into the store and attack her.

A manager came from the office and approached the drive-through area. The dog then calmed almost instantly. The employee said, "That's a miracle"; the manager agreed, adding jokingly, "Cujo was after you," referring to a dog in a novel written by Stephen King.

Then the manager saw me standing near and expressed concern, saying that might cause something bad to happen. I didn't know what that meant, and neither did the person at the drive-through window.

The employee wondered if the dog would return to attack her. The manager said something like, "No, that dog is gone. With James it happens at a higher level. Maybe something will happen to Stephen King, who wrote that book, *Cujo*. It shouldn't have been written."

If my memory is correct, soon afterward, either the same day or the next day, author Stephen King was seriously injured in a terrible accident. I feel terrible about this and wonder how and why it happened.

On February 28, 1958, when I was 25 days old, what was then the worst school bus accident in United States history occurred in Floyd County, Kentucky. A school bus collided with a tow truck then ran off the road into a rain-swollen river. The bus driver and 26 of the students on board drowned.

Though my family lived in Harlan County, Kentucky, then, my mom and dad met when they lived in Floyd County and both sets of my grandparents lived in Floyd County at the time of that accident.

Many years after that tragedy, I heard someone telling someone else that the reason for the accident allegedly was something like, "They tried to kill the witch's baby and missed." That individual seemed to be implying that some persons tried to kill me and somehow killed many other innocent children instead.

I still remember this and wonder if it is true that the accident happened as a misguided effort to kill me. I pray for God's perfect will for everyone and feel terrible about what happened to the persons who drowned after that bus plunged into the Big Sandy River in Floyd County, Kentucky.

Chapter 31: My Determination to Write and Being Prevented

I can be stubborn sometimes. One day sometime during the years 1993-1997 while living with my dad and mom in Jenkins, Kentucky, I felt frustrated because my writing was progressing so slowly. I determined to write no matter what.

I sat down at my computer to write. But as I began typing into my computer the electrical power went off. I learned later that a car had hit a utility pole. I got out my manual typewriter to write with, but I had lost my train of thought.

Was this a coincidence? Or, was some spiritual force upset about my writing?

I hope that in the future when my writing is going poorly that I will seek to pray for guidance instead of seeking to progress on with determination. My determination to write apparently led to someone experiencing a car accident.

I pray for God's perfect will to be done regarding all things, including my writing.

Chapter 32: Berlin Wall Fell on the Day I Arrived in Washington, D.C. for a Visit

The primary purpose of my first visit to Washington, D.C., was to attend the National Conference on the United States and the United Nations, held at the Ramada Renaissance Hotel at Techworld November 9-11, 1989.

At the time, I was a member of The United Nations Association of the United States of America (UNA-USA). UNA-USA is an organization of people that seeks to support the United Nations in various ways.

I lived in Lexington, Kentucky, and served as the newsletter editor (a volunteer position) for the Bluegrass Chapter of UNA-USA. I occasionally wrote articles/editorials, but I mainly compiled into newsletter format materials others submitted. They did a marvelous job of providing well-written material in a timely manner at an appropriate length for the newsletter.

International and intercultural things fascinated me. I decided to attend the National Conference on the United States and the United Nations, which was being held in Washington, D.C., and even allowed for some time after the conference to visit some D.C. tourist sites.

To my amazement, on the day I arrived in Washington, D.C. the Berlin Wall came down, the first day (November 9, 1989) of the three-day conference

Was this planned? Was it a coincidence? Either way, it was wonderful. Praise God!

On a trip to New York City about 20 years ago I got the opportunity to see and speak briefly with Walter Cronkite. The way it happened seems like a very unusual coincidence.

It was about twilight, and I was walking somewhere between the Times Square area and the United Nations area. I was amazed at how deserted the streets were. I could see for blocks and saw no one. I did not even see a moving vehicle.

Then a car drove up and parked at the curb beside the sidewalk in front of a hotel some feet in front of where I was on the sidewalk. A lady got out of the passenger side and went into the hotel.

Then the driver of the car got out and walked over. I recognized it was Walter Cronkite. I said "Good evening, Mr. Cronkite," and I think he said good evening to me.

I think those were the only words spoken verbally, but I have been gifted to sometimes be able to read thoughts from others, and in some cases I think they deliberately convey their unspoken thoughts to me. In addition to the spoken words, Cronkite apparently inaudibly conveyed some other thoughts to me.

Among other things, he stated that he had never seen the streets of New York so deserted. He indicated that he couldn't see the bridges from there but that he believed that all over New York City people were probably leaving, and that if I stood there long enough he would have to leave, too. He thought I might someday be "the last living boy in New York" and wondered if I'd heard of the Simon & Garfunkel song by that title.

He added the thought that at one time he was considered by some to be "the most trusted man in America" and that although it wasn't true then or now, that I might be. He indicated that I was the most trusted man he had ever met. I was flattered though I considered it hyperbole.

He inaudibly conveyed a few other thoughts, including that if my name was James and I was from Kentucky it would be good for me to return to Kentucky and stay there, before entering the hotel. I still remember that brief encounter and what I perceived as inaudible thoughts conveyed to me by Cronkite as a highlight of my New York trip.

Chapter 34: My Psychiatric Hospitalizations and What I Learned from Them

During the period of 1993-1996 I (the author of this book) was psychiatrically hospitalized briefly a few times here in Kentucky, and also received outpatient psychiatric treatment for what some psychiatrists considered a mild psychiatric disorder. Other psychiatrists, I think, considered me normal.

I think even normal people can think, speak, and act irrationally when under a lot of stress. At any rate, even the psychiatrists who diagnosed me seemed to think mine was at most a minor case.

For a period of time I took lithium for a diagnosis of a mild case of bipolar disorder. I began taking a lower dose without experiencing any problems. Then, on a follow-up visit, an enlightened psychiatrist formally reduced my prescribed dosage by 50%. Soon afterward, I completely stopped taking it. Since 1996 I have not taken any lithium or any other drug for mental illness, and I feel fine.

The root of my problem came when I began speaking inappropriately about certain things I witnessed. This led to a series of events that led to my psychiatric hospitalizations. It was a trying period. I could probably write a book about this.

However, I was blessed immeasurably during this period of 1993-1996, and I am blessed immeasurably now, too. That period was stressful at the time, but it was a good learning experience.

What did me more good than the psychiatric hospitalizations themselves, I think, was the physical relocation out of the towns I lived in (Nicholasville, then Jenkins) to the cities/larger towns where the two psychiatric hospitals that I was admitted to were located (Lexington and Hazard).

Also, in my humble opinion, preparing and eating a nutritious diet, exercising regularly such as by taking a nice morning walk, reading uplifting books and/or devotional material, and living in a larger more cosmopolitan city, as well as working at a fulfilling career and helping others can do more good for many than a psychiatric hospital can.

When I moved from Nicholasville to Jenkins in 1993 to live with my dad and mom, I wanted to prepare my own food, wash my own dishes, and wash my own clothes. Had mom let me do this initially, I think it would have helped prevent many of the problems. And when she finally did allow me to do so, I think it was a key part of helping me overcome the mental illness.

I am not a medical professional, so I can't give medical advice. But I feel having a good support group of friends and relatives is a key, too.

Perhaps most important in my case, if I had been ". . . speaking the truth in love. . ." as Ephesians 4:15 (KJV) states, I likely could have avoided upsetting others, which set off the chain reaction of events that led to my psychiatric hospitalizations. I now try harder to be truthful in a loving way.

Once when I was in my apartment in Lexington, Kentucky, I was trying to decide between two alternatives. I decided flipping a coin might be an effective way to make a decision.

I tossed a coin. Instead of it landing either "heads" or "tails," the coin landed on its edge. I was astonished.

I laughed and looked at the coin carefully. It seemed like a normal coin.

I flipped a coin again, either that coin or another coin. This coin flip also resulted in the coin landing on its edge.

Then I heard an inaudible voice say something like, "Now stop flipping coins and pray."

I took the advice of that voice. I prayed to receive guidance about what to decide regarding the two alternatives.

As a result of this, I decided that flipping a coin is not a random way to decide between two alternatives. I also gained a new appreciation for the importance of prayer.

Maybe after others read what I wrote about this experience they will gain a new appreciation for the importance of prayer, too. I hope so.

Several years ago when I was working a job in a restaurant at a location here in Kentucky that I won't disclose, one day when I was off work, I was concerned about a possible malfunction in one of the vats used to prepare food that might impact the store after the time when it was turned on to warm up for lunch. I prayed about it.

Just as I was praying, there was an electrical outage that affected much of the town I lived in at the time, including the vat a couple of miles away. I feel that somehow my concern about the malfunction and praying about it led to the brief power outage. I know that the power outage affected the restaurant, because I phoned them about the vat right after my prayer, during the power outage.

If I remember correctly, I had prayed for God's perfect will regarding the malfunctioning vat. But perhaps not. At any rate, I think this points out the importance of choosing one's words carefully when praying.

I remember an occasion when I was in a Sunday School class in a church here in Kentucky, and the teacher (in my opinion) deliberately told a lie. I looked at her intently to let her know that I knew she was lying and that I didn't like her lying.

She seemed very frightened. She wore several pieces of jewelry and began rubbing one or more pieces of her jewelry with one or both hands. If I remember correctly, she wore a necklace, bracelets, a ring, earrings, and maybe other jewelry.

Then she said something like, "If he focuses his eyes on me, all this jewelry won't do me a bit of good. I'll fall down on the floor laughing, and I won't get up. Well, I won't be laughing, but I will fall on the floor and I won't get up. I wonder if he knows the story of Ananias and Sapphira." After a few seconds, she added something like, "He doesn't know how to focus them. Good."

I didn't (and still don't) know how to focus my eyes that way. And I don't desire to harm others. I seek to love everyone.

But this incident helped convince me that the Bible story of Ananias and Sapphira (in Acts 5:1-10) is basically true. I believe God enabled Peter to focus his eyes on Ananias, then Sapphira, in a way that led them to be struck dead.

After this incident, my Sunday School teacher mumbled to herself something like, "it would probably be better if he [me] did not come back to my [her] Sunday School class." And I think I always or virtually always attended another Sunday School class afterward. But I've never forgotten that incident.

I find it strange but true that each of us seems disabled in certain ways, but seems blessed with special gifts in other ways to compensate. We human beings are born with certain abilities and develop others during our lives. But we come in various shapes and sizes. And we all have what could be termed disabilities, of some type.

Personally, I am gifted in various ways, but there are other areas where I am for all practical purposes what some would call handicapped. For example, I am a terrible artist. I have difficulty drawing even a stick figure. During my elementary school years, I broke down in tears one night, frustrated by being unable to draw something for a homework assignment.

In high school, I was not a good biology lab person. I had difficulty identifying parts when dissecting animals or looking at things under a microscope and drawing them. Fortunately, I had a knowledgeable biology lab partner.

I also am not very good at memorizing things, such as a long poem.

At a surveying camp that was a required course in the mining engineering program at the University of Kentucky, I was perhaps the worst student in that field class. I also may have been the worst student in the hands-on portion of a mine safety training class that was required at the beginning of a summer job after my freshman year of college.

But, through the grace of God, I do read and write reasonably well. I also did well in school in arithmetic, as well as several other subjects. I was arguably the best math student and best spelling student in my class at each school I attended from elementary school through high school.

I have often heard others condemn certain people for being unable to do something. However, just because someone else can't do something you consider simple, doesn't mean they deserve condemnation. We all have certain weaknesses, areas where we may appear incompetent. But, we often (always?) are gifted in ways to compensate for our weaknesses.

When I was in the third grade, my mom and then my dad tried to teach me how to tie my shoelaces. Dad succeeded in teaching me how to tie them with one bow, but I did not learn how to tie my shoes with two bows until the summer before I started high school. I wore slip-on shoes during the latter years of elementary school. But I knew that in my high school freshman physical education class we had to wear gym shoes, and they were lace-up shoes. I knew that I would be very embarrassed if I couldn't tie my own shoes for gym class.

So I decided to practice tying my shoes. I allotted a few hours one day early that summer after eighth grade when I was home alone to practice tying a pair of dad's shoes. Fortunately, it was much easier than I'd expected. I taught myself how to tie shoes in a few minutes. I may still not tie them exactly the way others do or quite as quickly, but I can tie my shoelaces with two bows that look reasonably normal reasonably quickly.

I did reasonably well in all my classes in high school. In some subjects, I was perhaps the best student in the elementary schools and high schools I attended.

My freshman year in college I even tutored someone a bit in college algebra though I never took the course. However, I did not do well in calculus.

I try to treat everyone fairly (as dad and mom taught me). I was reasonably popular in elementary school and in high school. In fact, I was voted class president my freshman year in high school (though I admit I did very little as class president). My senior year in high school I was voted male most likely to succeed, in addition to receiving the math award and Kiwanis award, as well as being selected valedictorian. God and others deserve the credit for my successes though.

I find it wonderful that persons who are disabled in one area are especially gifted in another. This is true for all of us. We all are gifted in multiple ways, and we are all disabled in other ways.

I firmly believe that each of us can learn something from any other person and that each of us can teach any other person something. Therefore, I hope we will all seek to help one another and to learn from one another without judging or condemning anyone. I know that doing this is easier written about than achieved, but I am seeking to do so and hope to try even harder to do so in the future. I hope you will, too.

Once, when I was in my mom's living room in Jenkins, Kentucky, with one particular relative and some other relatives, as I was looking at that one particular relative, suddenly a large bright white cross appeared in front of me that for some reason reminded me of the Transfiguration in the Bible gospels.

I don't know the cause of the large white cross.

I also remember another occasion a week or so earlier when I was visiting a patient in a hospital room that had a cross on the wall in a southeastern Kentucky hospital, and I prayed focusing on the cross, and mom's cell phone rang (mom was also in the room visiting the patient), and it was the same relative phoning mom.

On a third occasion, perhaps a few years earlier, when I was visiting another relative in southeastern Kentucky, I thought about this particular relative, and the phone of the relative that I was visiting rang, and it was that relative phoning.

These three incidents involving the same relative seem very unusual, and to me are examples of cases where truth may seem stranger than fiction.

Once when I visited the church that my dad and mom belonged to in southeastern Kentucky, as I walked in I saw the people who had arrived early for the church services moving rapidly back and forth. Perhaps they were moving some items. But I couldn't tell the purpose of all their movements and had never seen the church members moving back and forth in such a rapid manner on any of my other visits.

I wondered the reason for it. I asked at least a couple of people, but I either didn't get an answer or didn't understand the answer. Perhaps they were moving things around for some useful purpose, but I didn't recognize any organized movement. Personally, I just sat down as I normally did when I visited. (I was a member of another denomination, just visiting.)

Not long afterward (a few days later?), I saw our family Run Yourself Ragged® game on the stairway. I asked mom why it was there. I think mom said Barb (my sister) had borrowed it and just brought it back.

That could be mere coincidence, but that day at the church the people seemed to be running themselves ragged. Could there be some correlation between that game and the way the people behaved at church that day.

There have been other times when I behaved abnormally. I wonder what the cause of that was, too?

Chapter 41: October 19 Birthday of Friend Whose Dad Sold Stocks and Huge Stock Market Crash

On October 19, 1987, the stock market (the Dow Jones 30 Industrials Average) suffered its biggest one-day loss in history up to that time both in points and in percentage. The Dow Jones 30 Industrials dropped 508 points to close at 1738, a 22.6% decline.

A friend of mine told me her dad's career included the buying and selling of stocks. This huge stock market drop happened on her birthday (October 19). Was this a coincidence?

Years ago, Grady Nutt (a well-known ordained Southern Baptist minister, humorist, and television personality) visited the church where I attended at the time. He visited the college department Sunday School area and greeted us. As we exchanged greetings with him a person in front of me said something to him like, "I know you are someone famous, but I don't know who you are. May I ask?" Grady Nutt told them, then asked who they were. I think the person said they were not important, and Grady Nutt stated that yes, they were.

I made a comment similar to the one the other person had to Grady Nutt. Grady Nutt responded similarly to the way he had to the other person. And another Sunday School student said that because of my comment Grady Nutt was going to die and that it would happen soon.

I found that hard to believe. But soon afterward, Grady Nutt died unexpectedly, on November 23, 1982 in a plane crash.

I try to be more careful how I speak now.

Chapter 43: Three Uses of a Similar Name (Lilley, Lili, Lillia), Coincidence?

An October 17, 1996 7:52 p.m. journal entry I wrote mentioned three uses of a similar name (Lilley, Lili, and Lillia) in what may be an amazing coincidence.

(1)The note stated that my mom and her grandchildren Corey and Stachia were "planning to go on a field trip with the Burdine Christian School to Lilly [Lilley] Cornett Woods tomorrow [October 18, 1996], weather permitting." Lilley Cornett Woods is a nature preserve in Letcher County, Kentucky, not far from where they lived.

(2)My journal entry also stated that "the evening news reported that tropical storm Lilly [Lili] became a hurricane last night."

(3)The note in my journal also stated that "Lilly Dingus passed away either today or yesterday apparently since they are having visitation for her at the funeral home tomorrow night. God works in mysterious ways." According to her obituary in the October 23, 1996 Whitesburg, Kentucky, *Mountain Eagle* newspaper, "She was the oldest member of the Burdine Free Will Baptist Church." That obituary listed her as "Lillia B. Dingus, 93."

Was the occurrence of these three similar names in different situations in such a short time frame a coincidence?

I moved from Nicholasville, Kentucky, back to Jenkins, Kentucky, in 1993. The next year (in 1994) a southeastern Kentucky coal miner named James Keith Gibson was killed in a mining accident.

I have a mining engineering degree and worked two summers in the mining industry. It seems unusual that the year after I moved back to the coal mining area in southeastern Kentucky that a coal miner with the same first name and surname as me died in an accident.

James Gibson is a relatively common name. Still, I found this very unusual. Was this death a coincidence?

Chapter 45: Nearby Neighbor Girls With Same Birth Date as Me in Two Towns

In two consecutive towns in which my family lived in southeastern Kentucky, we had neighbors living nearby with a daughter who had the same birthday as me (February 3). In one town, that girl's family moved there after we did. In the other town, I'm not sure if that family moved there after we did or before, but mom said they moved there after we did.

In each case they were arguably the girls living nearest to our house, though in one case two other families with daughters lived a comparable distance away. In the other case I think one other family that included a daughter lived a comparable distance away from our family.

Was this just a coincidence that these two girls shared the same birthday as me?

As a boy I enjoyed having a speedometer and odometer on my bicycle. On more than one occasion, the cable broke on it, and I had to have it replaced.

On one occasion when it apparently broke, I was bicycling rapidly on an unpaved road near the house where we lived in Pike County, Kentucky. I prayed that if God would repair my speedometer I would have faith in God.

Miraculously it seemed, the bicycle speedometer began working again. I am sorry to say that I then began thinking maybe it was coincidence, etc., and my faith in God failed. Then the bicycle speedometer stopped working again, permanently this time.

Was the bicycle speedometer repaired miraculously through my prayer, then the repair "cancelled" due to my lack of faith. Or perhaps the bicycle cable was only partially broken, and a bump jarred it enough to work briefly again before permanent failure. There is probably no scientific way to know for sure. But, it certainly seems unusual that the speedometer began working again right after my prayer.

My faith in God has wavered numerous times since that incident. And I was an agnostic during much of my childhood. But I do have faith in God now.

I lived with my dad and mom in Jenkins, Kentucky, for approximately four years during 1993-1997. During some if not all of this time they owned a refrigerator with a water dispenser in it that dispensed cold water when a lever was pressed, without the need to open the refrigerator door.

A person could just put a cup or glass up below the spout, push it against a lever and water would flow down into the cup. One day as I was using it, I heard my dad somewhere else in the house groan in pain. I stopped to listen. He didn't say anything more.

Then as I began pushing the lever again, dad groaned again. This happened at least three times. Dad's groaning in apparent pain and my pushing the lever seemed correlated somehow even though he was many feet away and out of sight of me and the refrigerator, so I stopped using the water dispenser, even though when I had hollered to ask dad if he was all right, he replied that he was.

Mom was in the kitchen with me and said it was coincidence. But, I'm not convinced it was coincidence. It seemed uncanny.

After I moved to Lexington, Kentucky, in 1976 to become a student at the University of Kentucky, the following two winters (1976-77 and 1977-78) were two of the three coldest in recorded Kentucky history according to the Kentucky Almanac (see page 369, *Clark's Kentucky Almanac and Book of Facts 2006*, copyright 2005).

I moved to Jenkins, Kentucky, from Nicholasville, Kentucky, in 1993. During the following winter, in January 1994, a severe winter storm resulted in Kentucky's governor closing interstate highways in Kentucky for a few days.

When I moved back to Lexington, Kentucky, from Jenkins, Kentucky, in 1997, the following winter we had a huge snowfall [spread over three days, I think] in Lexington that was probably the largest snowfall in recorded history for Lexington.

What caused these unusual weather conditions following my moves? Were they coincidences?

On January 18, 1996 (my mom's birthday is January 18) I went to the Jenkins, Kentucky, hospital to get my medical records for a previous visit to them for treatment.

Coincidentally?, later during the same day that I got my medical records, the former mayor of Jenkins, James F. "Chum" Tackett, was involved in a fight at a middle school game, according to the January 26, 1996 issues of the Whitesburg *Mountain Eagle* and Letcher County *Community Press*. Those newspaper articles provide more details about the fight, and I am not stating that the former mayor was at fault in the fight. The other individual may have been responsible.

Was this a coincidence?

Chapter 50: Dr. D. James Kennedy Speech and President Kennedy

During the early 1990s, I went to hear the well-known Presbyterian minister, Dr. D. James Kennedy, speak at Southland Christian Church as part of a conference. I did not pay to attend the conference itself. However, Dr. Kennedy's speech was free, so I attended it.

Before the speech, I took time to have a devotional time in the lower level of the church. After exiting the building following my devotional time and going to get in line to attend the speech itself, I was amazed that the person in front of me in the line of perhaps hundreds of people was John C. Depriest, the pastor at the Burdine Free Will Baptist Church in Burdine, Kentucky. My mom and dad were baptized at the Burdine Free Will Baptist Church while I was a college student and joined that church. It surprised me that Brother John (as he was commonly known) had come to the conference. But, it was an even bigger surprise that he happened to be directly in front of me among all those people there.

During his talk, Dr. D. James Kennedy appeared to focus directly at me at least once and on that occasion say something like, "I don't know about you, but I'm getting a headache." I got the feeling that I was inadvertently causing him to get a headache. Perhaps he hypnotized many/most persons and was only speaking to me when he said this.

On a later occasion, sometime after the conference, I got the impression from an inaudible voice that I was Dr. D. James Kennedy's man in Kentucky, whatever that means. I also got the impression that somehow I as a five-year-old boy on November 22, 1963 when President John F. Kennedy was assassinated, and Dr. D. James Kennedy were connected. However, I never met President Kennedy and only saw Dr. D. James Kennedy that one time at his speech. Below I discuss two other things that may be related to this at least indirectly.

First, in the October 21, 1996 "My Turn" column in *Newsweek* Magazine, motion picture director Oliver Stone alleged that "new evidence" indicated President Kennedy had intended "to withdraw all American forces from Vietnam." Stone stated that details are in *JFK and Vietnam* by John Newman, professor of history at the University of Maryland.

Second, I remember someone at a meeting I attended about three decades ago mentioning various U.S. government persons who served in various agencies around the world gathering for a meeting in Texas on November 22, 1963 that he attended, and that President Kennedy also attended, on the same day that the President was shot. This individual stated that the meeting was relatively short. He also indicated that the meeting subdivided into smaller groups for a period of time, and that since he was relatively young and inexperienced, he was not in the main subgroup(s).

I'm guessing the meeting was held in Fort Worth before the President traveled to Dallas. Apparently a large number of important U.S. personnel from around the world attended this meeting. Did that signify it was an important conference? What was the purpose of the meeting? Did the President seek major foreign policy changes? Could he have been planning to end the war in Vietnam? Did he desire to eliminate or greatly reduce a lot of other international interventions, such as those the U.S. had been involved in during the 1950s and early 1960s? I don't know the answers to these questions.

The events I described in this chapter may not be related at all. They may be coincidences, but who knows?

At any rate, personally I would love for all conflicts to be resolved peacefully and fairly. I would love to see an end to wars and violent conflicts. If we all seek to listen to the viewpoints of others who disagree with us, then seek fair and just solutions instead of our own selfish desires, I think that this is possible. It may take miraculous help from God to attain this, but I certainly believe that it is possible.

This chapter may seem out of place in the book, but I feel that it is an important one that is worth including. To me, one of the strange but true things in the United States is the unusual choice we sometimes seem to make when we vote for a person for President, Congress, or some other office.

We often talk about voting for a person with integrity, wisdom, etc. But it seems that we often vote for persons who are corrupt individuals. Any person running for office who seeks campaign donations in exchange for favors, supports the platform of his political party (Democratic, Republican, etc.) whether it is right or wrong, lies, steals, takes advantage of a position of political power to engage in sexual lust, etc., seems to be a poor choice, other things being equal.

With over 300 million persons in the United States, one would think we could find and develop persons of integrity to take office and make things better. However, sometimes it seems that the political party leaders, persons already in office, witches, Freemasons, or whatever with power, seem determined to drag honest people down, to get something on them to control them, and to put and keep dishonest persons in office that they can control for their own selfish purposes. They sometimes seem to want to cover up for their "buddies" when they are wrong, and to work against those who are not their "buddies," even when they are right.

I firmly believe that society as a whole will be much better off if we all seek to do the right things and to put the right people in the right positions regardless of their political party, etc.

The term honest politician may sometimes seem almost like an oxymoron. But I am confident that at the town, county, state, national, and international level that there are a lot of dedicated public servants holding office that we need to support and in many cases promote to higher level offices. I think it is strange (but true) that so few of these quality people get promoted up to top level positions. Let's seek to do a better job of helping these quality persons (and all persons) develop their skills and reach their potential, for the good of society as a whole.

I am considering running for President of the United States myself in 2020 or 2024 if I remain alive and healthy if we don't get better qualified persons to run than the major party candidates on the ballot in November 2016—Donald Trump and Hillary Clinton. My campaign slogan may be "Seeking 20/20 Vision for 2020" if I run in 2020.

However, among the millions of persons eligible to run, I hope and pray that someone better qualified than I am will run—and win. Perhaps in the 2016 election one of the other candidates running for President was better qualified than Trump or Clinton, but didn't get the support needed to win.

I know I would need to acquire a lot more knowledge and wisdom and be willing and able to put that knowledge and wisdom into practice in order to be qualified.

I hope and pray that the best qualified persons run for and obtain job openings of all types, including the office of President of the United States.

I feel that God provides each of us with special gifts. My desire is to do God's perfect will—indeed, for all of us to do God's perfect will. Are some (or all) of us gifted with some form of special hearing ability and speech that conveys long distances under certain circumstances? Do our eyes have special powers that can be developed and used for exceptionally good purposes? If I am blessed with a special gift of God, I desire to use it properly for good.

I feel that I have experienced an unusually high number of events that are difficult to explain. Perhaps, though, many persons (or maybe all of us) experience at least some of these very unusual events. I don't know if I or anyone will ever completely understand them.

The closer we get to total devotion to the highest righteous authority, God, and God's perfect righteous will, the better the outcome of these "unusual event" occasions will be, as I see it. I pray for God's perfect will to be done in all things.

Lots of other unusual things have happened to me, and I may write more about them, too, if I feel God desires me to. My desire is to write according to God's timetable, in a positive way that does good, in the way God desires, which requires God's leadership.

About the Author

This is James E. Gibson's second book. He self-published his first book, *True Christianity: It May Not Be What You Think*, in 2014 (second edition 2015, third edition 2017). He's also written numerous articles for websites, including Google Blogger, Newsvine, Yahoo! Voices (and its predecessor Associated Content), and Helium.

James is a former agnostic who became a Christian during his college years at the University of Kentucky. He holds B.S. degrees in mining engineering and civil engineering, as well as an MBA.

He has loved to read and write since childhood. As a bivocational freelance writer, he has worked a variety of second jobs to help keep the bills paid while fulfilling his dream of developing a writing career.

A series of unusual events/coincidences and the author's inappropriate way of speaking about them led to a series of things that resulted in a few brief psychiatric hospitalizations for him and outpatient psychiatric treatment during 1993 to 1996. But he was blessed immeasurably during that time and is now as well.

The author is a very ecumenical nondenominational Christian who seeks to love everyone. He would love for all persons to live happier, healthier, longer, more fruitful lives and feels that as we come closer to practicing true Christianity, we come closer to reaching this ideal, too.

Order Form and Ordering Information

If you would like an additional copy (or copies) of this book you can order or buy it (or them) from a bookstore, Amazon.com, and other sources. You may also use the order form below to order one copy shipped to a location in the contiguous U.S. (not Alaska or Hawaii).

On all orders, please add $4 for shipping and handling. Kentucky residents please add 6% state sales tax to the total cost.

Sorry, no returns allowed. Prices subject to change without notice. Payment accepted by check or money order. Please allow 30 days for delivery. Thanks! Books will be shipped from the printer.

If you desire to order two or more copies, please email me at jamesegibson@gmail.com for prices and terms, or write me at the Post Office Box address below. If you write my Post Office Box address, please enclose a self-addressed, stamped envelope. Thanks!

Also, you may email or write for prices and terms to buy a copy of my other book, *True Christianity: It May Not Be What You Think*.

Please send me one copy of *Several True (I Think) Stories: Can Truth Be Stranger Than Fiction?*, Second Edition, for a price of $11.00 + $4 for shipping and handling + $0.90 Kentucky state sales tax if being mailed to a Kentucky address (omit the $0.90 if your mailing address is outside of Kentucky).

Here is my check or money order for $15.90 (or $15.00 if your mailing address is outside Kentucky.)

Name...

Address..

City/State...

Zip Code...

E-mail address (optional)...

Please make your check or money order out to James E. Gibson. Mail orders to: James E. Gibson, P.O. Box 54868, Lexington, KY 40555-4868 Thanks! Enjoy God's blessings!

www.ingramcontent.com/pod-product-compliance
Lightning Source LLC
Chambersburg PA
CBHW062119040426
42336CB00041B/2036